AARON COPLAND

IN THE BEGINNING

for mixed chorus
a cappella with
mezzo-soprano solo

BOOSEY&HAWKES

AN IMAGEM COMPANY

DISTRIBUTED BY

HAL•LEONARD®

IN THE BEGINNING

For Mixed Chorus a cappella
with Mezzo-Soprano Solo

Text from Genesis
Chap. I: 1 - II: 7

Aaron Copland
(1947)

Written for the Harvard Symposium on Music Criticism, May 1947

* At the conductor's discretion, the piano part may be used in performance as an aid to the singers.

LCB-14

Printed in U.S.A.

4

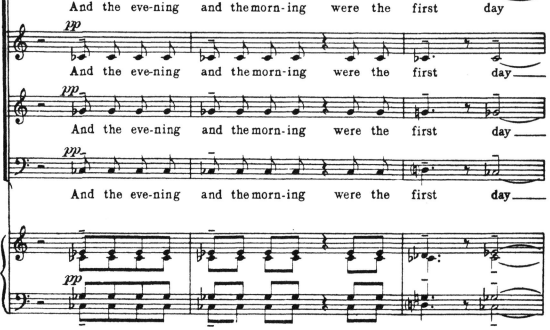

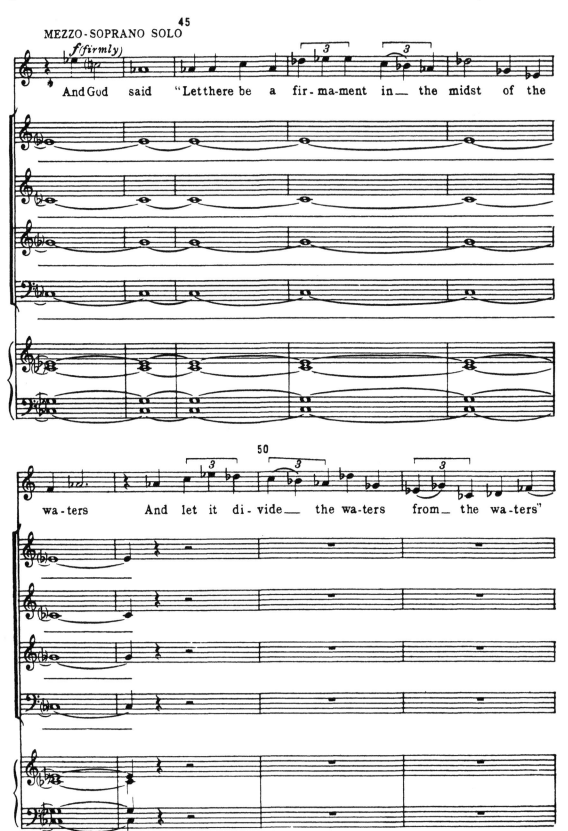

And God made the fir-ma-ment and di - vid-ed the wa - ters

And God made the fir-ma-ment and di-vid-ed the

55

And_ God made the fir-ma-ment and di - vid-ed the wa - ters

wa - ters And_ God made the fir-ma-ment and di-vid-ed the

And God made the fir-ma-ment and di-vid-ed the

And God made the fir-ma-ment and di-

8

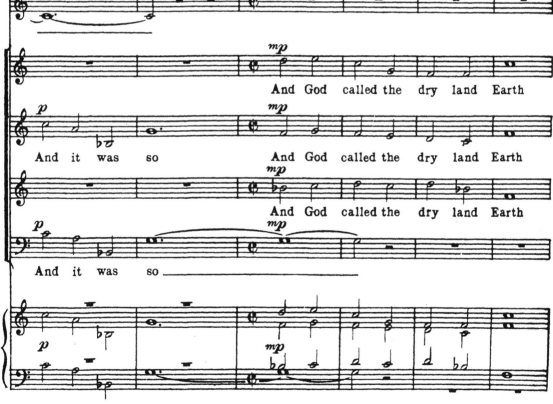

14

lights in the fir-ma-ment of the heav-en to di-vide the day from the

poco sf-mf

lights!

poco sf-mf

lights!

poco sf-mf

lights!

poco sf-mf

poco sf-mf

poco sf-mf

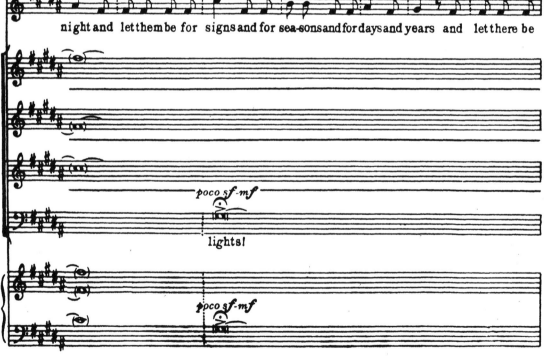

night and let them be for signs and for sea-sons and for days and years and let there be

poco sf-mf

lights!

poco sf-mf

signs and for sea-sons and for days and years and let there be

signs and for sea-sons and for days and years and let there be

lights ____

poco sf   poco sf   lights ____

lights ____

poco sf   lights ____

poco sf   poco sf   poco sf

poco sf

poco sf   poco sf   poco sf

lights in the fir-ma-ment of the heav-en to div-ide the

lights in the fir-ma-ment of the heav-en to div-ide the

lights ____

sim.   sim.

lights ____

sim lights ____

sim.

In The Beginning-

In The Beginning

rule o - ver the day and o - ver the night and to di-

rule o - ver the day and o - ver the night and to di-

rule o - ver the day and o - ver the night and to di-

rule o - ver the day and o - ver the night and to di-

vide the day from the dark - ness And God saw that it was good

vide the day from the dark - ness And God saw that it was good

vide the day from the dark - ness And God saw that it was good

vide the day from the dark - ness And God saw that it was good

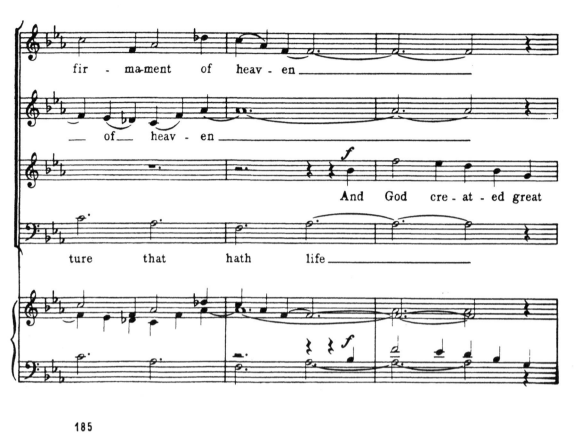

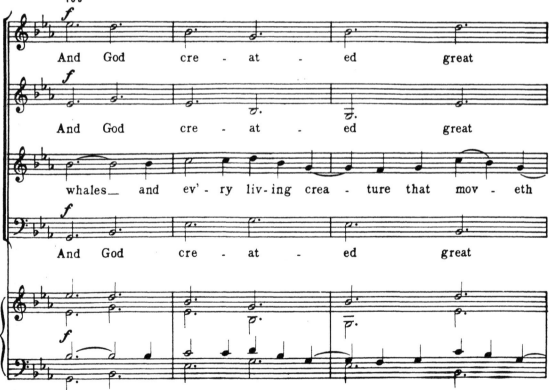

30

34

In The Beginning-55

38

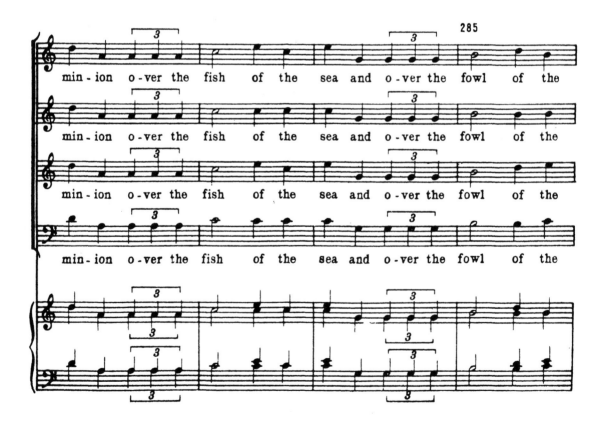

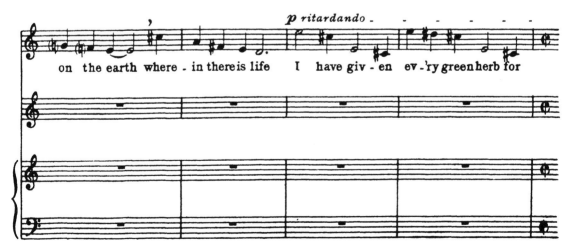

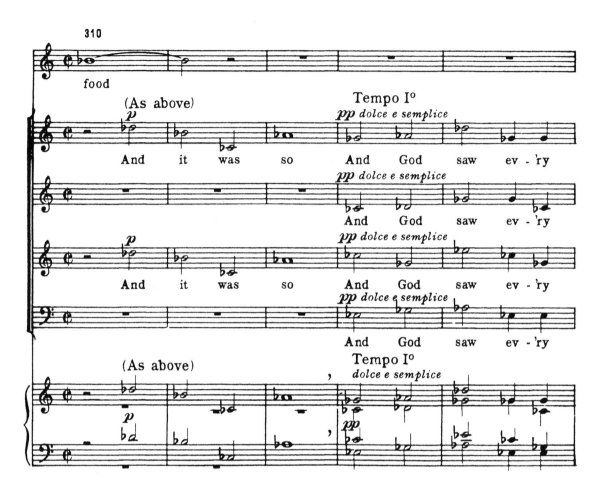

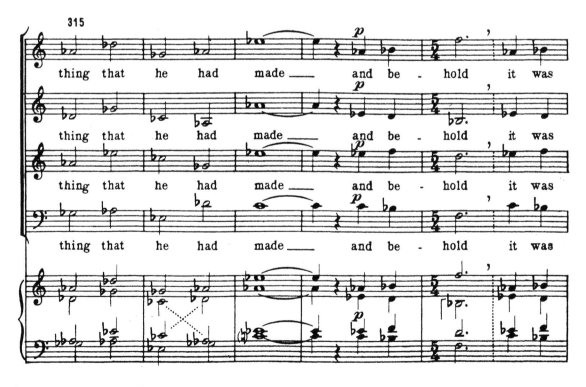

50

345

sanc - ti - fied it _____ be-cause that in it he had

sanc - ti - fied it _____ be-cause that in it he had

sanc - ti - fied it be-cause that in it he had rest - ed ___

be-cause that in it he had rest - ed ___

poco rit.

rest - ed from all his work which God cre - a - ted and

rest - ed from all his work which God cre - a - ted and

___ from all his work which God cre - a - ted and

___ from all his work which God cre - a - ted and

350
MEZZO-SOPRANO SOLO
(rather hurriedly)

These are the gen-er-a-tions of the heav-ens and of the

made / made / made / made

earth when they were cre-a-ted in the day that the Lord God made the earth and the

heav_ens and ev'_ry plant of the field be fore it was in the

earth and ev'-ry herb of the field be fore it grew__

380
Broadly (allarg.)
breath of life and man be-came a liv-ing
breath of life and man be-came a liv-ing
breath of life and man be-came a liv-ing
breath of life and man be-came a liv-ing
Broadly (allarg.)
Very broadly
385
(long)
soul, and man be-came a liv-ing soul, a liv-ing soul.
soul, and man be-came a liv-ing soul, a liv-ing soul.
soul, and man be-came a liv-ing soul, a liv-ing soul.
soul, and man be-came a liv-ing soul, a liv-ing soul.
Very broadly
(long)